Islands in the Sun

A Guidebook to the Caribbean

Alan Trussell-Cullen

CELEBRATION PRESS
Pearson Learning Group

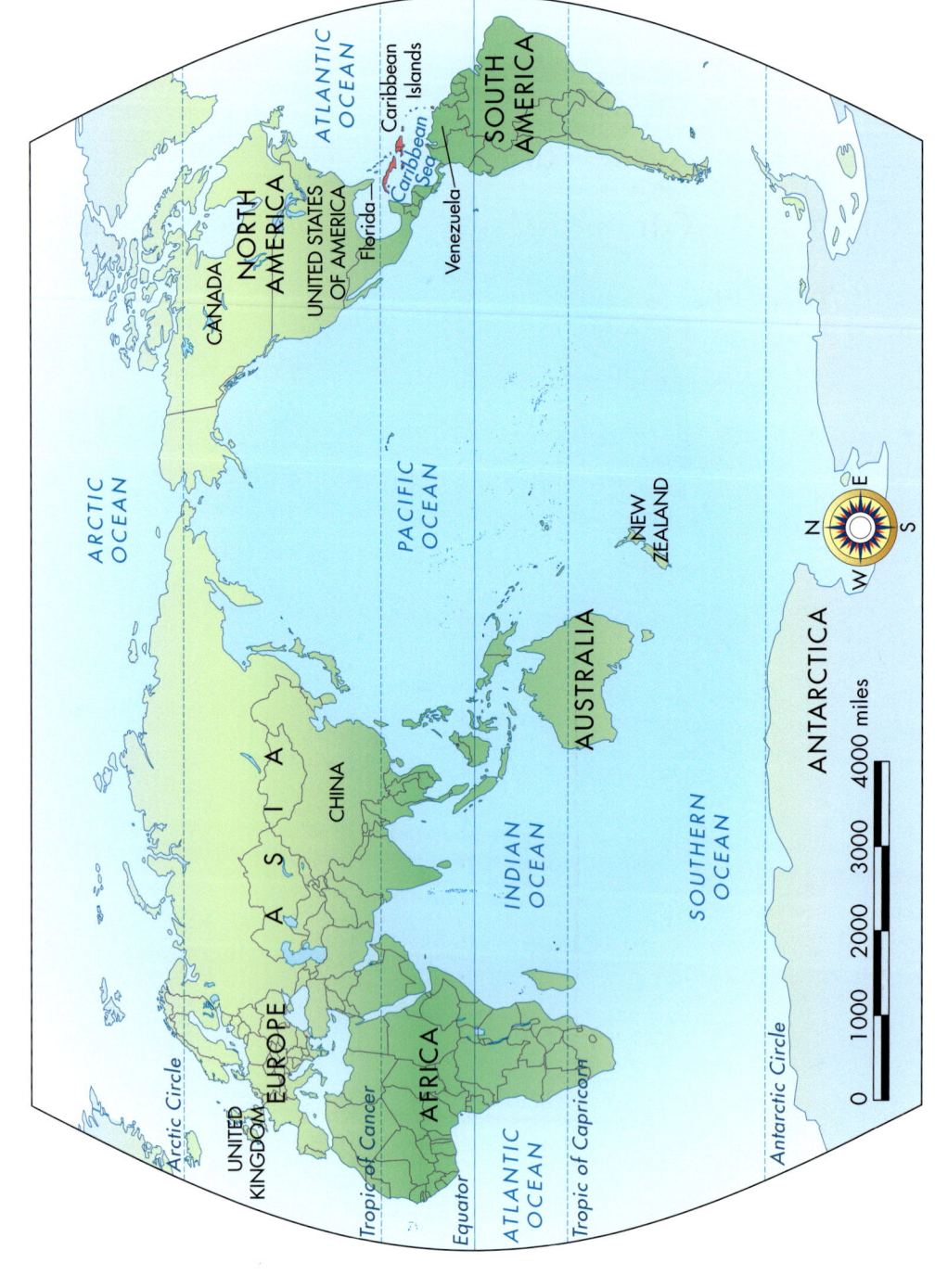

Contents

Islands of the Caribbean	4
Where Is the Caribbean?	6
The Weather	8
History	10
White Gold!	12
Slavery	13
Caribbean Timeline	14
The Nineteenth Century to the Present	15
People of the Caribbean	16
The Western Islands of the Caribbean	18
The Eastern Islands of the Caribbean	20
So Much to Enjoy!	22
Glossary	24
Index	24

Islands of the Caribbean

Beach at Tobago

Where would you like to go for a vacation? How about somewhere that is hot and tropical all year round, with golden beaches, clear blue seas, and a colorful history? How about a place where people dance and sing and love to have a good time?

Sounds like paradise, doesn't it? For thousands of vacationers from all around the world, the islands of the Caribbean are indeed a vacation paradise!

Diving with a shark, Cayman Islands

Caribbean steel band, playing **calypso** music

The island groups of the Caribbean Sea form an archipelago known as the West Indies. The West Indies archipelago has also been called the "Antilles".

Where Is the Caribbean?

Islands of the Caribbean

The Caribbean Sea lies north of the equator, midway between North America and South America. There are thousands of islands in the Caribbean Sea.

Some of the islands are large with many people living on them and some are tiny uninhabited rocky **outcrops**. Together these islands form an **arc** that stretches for 2,485 miles from the United States in North America to Venezuela in South America.

The islands of the Caribbean Sea may be divided into the western islands and the eastern islands.

The western islands include Cuba, the Cayman Islands, Jamaica, the Dominican Republic, and Haiti.

The eastern islands include Puerto Rico, the Virgin Islands, French Antilles, Grenada, Barbados, Trinidad, and Tobago.

Harbor at Saint Lucia in the eastern Caribbean

The Weather

Beach at Saint Johns

The islands of the Caribbean enjoy warm weather all year round because they are so close to the equator. However, it can be chilly at night and very early in the morning. It can also be very humid.

In the Caribbean region, there tend to be two main seasons. There is a rainy season from May through October, followed by a dry season from November through April.

There is one other season in the Caribbean—the hurricane season. During this season, which falls between June and November, there are violent rainstorms.

A Local Rhyme Explains the Hurricane Season

June: Too soon
July: Stand by
August: A must
September: Remember
October: All over!

Hurricane Mitch caused tidal waves on Grand Cayman Island in 1998.

History

A market scene at Santo Domingo, in the Caribbean, in 1800

People have been living in the Caribbean region for more than 5,000 years. The first inhabitants were the Ciboney people who were nomadic **hunter-gatherers**. Later the peaceful Arawak people arrived from South America, and then the warlike Caribs also came from South America.

The first European to set eyes on the islands of the Caribbean was the Italian navigator Christopher Columbus in 1492. Columbus thought he had found a sea route to the East Indies. That's how the Caribbean region came to be called the West Indies. We know now that Columbus was wrong! In fact, he was about 4,000 miles away from the East Indies, which was on the other side of the world!

A statue of Christopher Columbus

  Columbus was followed by many Spanish adventurers and settlers who came to **plunder** the wealth of the Caribbean. They shipped their gold and treasure back to Europe in slow-moving, heavily loaded vessels that soon became easy targets for pirates.

  The English, French, and Dutch also became interested in this region and claimed different islands as their **colonies**.

White Gold!

In the 1630s, Dutch farmers introduced sugar cane to the Caribbean. It grew well in the tropical **climate** of the region. The farmers became very rich because sugar sold for a very high price in Europe. In those days, sugar was so valuable it became known as "white gold". Sugar cane is still important in the Caribbean.

Workers cut sugar cane from a field and load it onto oxen carts.

Slavery

A big labor force was needed to grow and harvest the sugar cane. Thousands of West African people were captured and taken to the Caribbean. The captive West Africans were sold to plantation owners and forced to work in the sugar cane plantations.

In the 1800s, slavery was finally outlawed and the slaves were eventually set free.

Workers cut sugar cane in the West Indies in the late 1800s.

Caribbean Timeline

An old painting of the Saint Lucia Islands in the Caribbean

2000 B.C.	Stone Age Ciboney people settle the Caribbean.
300 B.C.	Arawaks arrive from South America.
A.D. 700	Carib Indians arrive from South America.
1492	Christopher Columbus arrives.
1500s	The Spanish plunder the islands' treasures.
1600s	The English, French, and Dutch establish colonies.
1630s	Sugar cane is introduced.
1700s	Thousands of West Africans are brought as slaves.
1800s	Slavery is banned.
1898	The United States takes possession of Puerto Rico.
1917	The United States buys the Virgin Islands from Denmark.
1960–70	Many islands become independent states.
2,000	The Caribbean is a world vacation destination.

The Nineteenth Century to the Present

After the Spanish-American War in 1898, the United States took possession of Puerto Rico, which had been a Spanish colony. In 1917, the United States bought the Virgin Islands from Denmark.

From the 1960s onward, many of the former European colonies became independent states.

Today the islands of the Caribbean have some of the most popular vacation resorts in the world.

A beach at a holiday resort in Tobago

People of the Caribbean

A market at Saint Georges in Grenada

A young girl in costume at a children's carnival in Trinidad

Many countries—Spain, England, Holland, France, the United States—have left their influence on the Caribbean. Although the islands are quite close to each other, the cultures and the ways people live are very different.

On neighboring islands, people speak different languages, eat different food, play different music, and have different festivals and ways of enjoying themselves.

That's why planning a vacation in the Caribbean can be so exciting.

The Western Islands of the Caribbean

Where would you like to go? What would you like to do? Choose an island from the western islands of the Caribbean.

CAYMAN ISLANDS

Visit the Cayman blue iguanas in the Queen Elizabeth Botanic Park.

DOMINICAN REPUBLIC

Go shopping in the central city market of Santo Domingo.

HAITI

Visit La Citadelle, a fort built by the last king of Haiti, Henri Christophe.

JAMAICA

Go hiking in the Blue Mountains, home of Blue Mountain coffee, one of the most famous coffees in the world.

Listen to **reggae** musicians and visit the Bob Marley Museum.

The Eastern Islands of the Caribbean

The eastern islands of the Caribbean are a wonder of glorious rain forest, heavenly beaches, and other tempting delights.

BARBADOS

The Andromeda Gardens are a haven for tropical plants.

FRENCH ANTILLES

The French Antilles, are also known as the French West Indies and are the islands in the Caribbean belonging to France.

Shop at a local market for fresh fish, fruit, and vegetables. Enjoy some **Creole** food.

GRENADA

Savour the wonderful spices grown in Grenada, which is known as the Spice Island.

PUERTO RICO

Explore the **limestone** caves of Rio Camuy Cave Park.

TRINIDAD AND TOBAGO

Wander through the rain forest of the Tobago Forest Reserve.

Enjoy the beaches of Trinidad.

21

So Much to Enjoy!

Yes, these islands in the sun are a wonderful cultural experience and a playground for all the senses.

colorful festivals to see

exciting sounds to hear

delicious foods to taste

exotic spices to smell

clear blue seas to touch

the magical sunsets
of the Caribbean

  No wonder vacationers from all around the world come to visit these islands in the sun!

Glossary

arc	a curved line
calypso	songs brought to the Caribbean by the West Africans
climate	normal weather conditions of a region
colonies	lands ruled by another country
Creole	a person born in the Caribbean whose family came from Africa or Europe
hunter-gatherers	people who provide food for a tribe by hunting and by gathering berries and roots
limestone	a rock used in building
outcrops	the rocky part of the landscape that juts out
plunder	to steal
reggae	a type of West Indian music made famous by Bob Marley

Index

Antilles	5	eastern islands	7, 20–21
Arawaks	10, 14	food	17, 20, 22
Caribbean Sea	5, 6, 7	hurricane season	9
Caribs	10, 14	rainy season	8
Christopher Columbus	11, 14	slavery	13, 14
Ciboney people	10, 14	sugar cane	12, 13, 14
climate	12	weather	8
culture	16, 22	West Indies	5, 10, 20
dry season	8	western islands	7, 18–19
East Indies	10	white gold	12